The ... Key Words Reading Scheme is based on the most commonly used words. Those used most often in the English language are introduced first—with other words of popular appeal to children. All the Key Words list is covered in the early books, and the later titles use further word lists to develop full reading fluency. The total number of different words which will be learned in the complete reading scheme is nearly two thousand. The gradual introduction of these words, frequent repetition and complete 'carry-over' from book to book, will ensure rapid learning.

The full-colour illustrations have been designed to create a desirable attitude towards learning— by making every child *eager* to read each title. Thus this attractive reading scheme embraces not only the latest findings in word frequency, but also the natural interests and activities of happy children.

Each book contains a list of the new words introduced.

W. MURRAY, the author of the Ladybird Key Words Reading Scheme, is an experienced headmaster, author and lecturer on the teaching of reading. He is co-author, with J. McNally, of 'Key Words to Literacy'—a teacher's book published by The Schoolmaster Publishing Co. Ltd.

THE LADYBIRD KEY WORDS READING SCHEME has 12 graded books in each of its three series—'a', 'b' and 'c'. As explained in the handbook 'Teaching Reading', these 36 graded books are all written on a controlled vocabulary, and take the learner from the earliest stages of reading to reading fluency.

The 'a' series gradually introduces and repeats new words. The parallel 'b' series gives the needed further repetition of these words at each stage, but in different context and with different illustrations.

The 'c' series is also parallel to the 'a' series, and supplies the necessary link with writing and phonic training.

An illustrated booklet—'Notes for Teachers'—can be obtained free from the publishers. This booklet fully explains the Key Words principle and the Ladybird Key Words Reading Scheme. It also includes information on the reading books, work books and apparatus available, and such details as the vocabulary loading and reading ages of all books.

BOOK 2c
The Ladybird Key Words Reading Scheme

I like to write

by W. MURRAY
with illustrations by MARTIN AITCHISON

Publishers: Ladybird Books Ltd . Loughborough
© Ladybird Books Ltd (formerly Wills & Hepworth Ltd) 1965
Printed in England

After reading Books 2a and 2b the learner should copy out and complete the following pages in an exercise book. Answers are given on Pages 46 to 51 for corrections, revision and testing.

Peter can write.

Jane c-- write.

I c-- write.

The answers are on Page 46

They can write.

T--- like to write.

T--- write for fun.

Peter writes for fun.

Jane writes f-- f--.

I like to write f-- f--.

The answers are on Page 46

8

I like to write

Peter, have
a sweet.
Have

I want t

Peter says,
Here you are, Jane.

Jane says,
Here y-- a-- , Peter.

Here y-- a-- ,
they say.

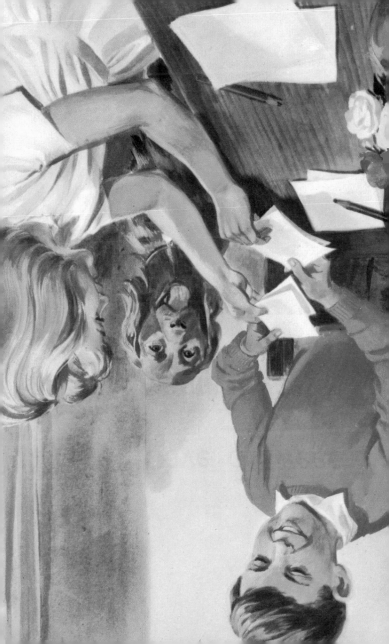

Peter, have a sweet.

H--- some sweets.

Have s--- s------,
Peter.

Peter, have
a sweet.
Have some
sweets.
Have some
sweets, Peter.

I want to fish.

I want to go to the water.

I w--- to g-- to the water, Jane.

The answers are on Page 47

Here comes Pat.

Here comes P--, the dog.

P-- c----- to Peter and Jane.

The answers are on Page 47

Here they come.

Here comes Peter.

Here c———— Jane.

Here c———— Pat.

Look here, Peter says.
Look here, he s——— .
The fish can jump.
L——, the f——— can
j———— .

The answers are on Page 48

The ball is in the water.

Go for it, says Peter to Pat.

G- for i-, h- says.

Pat jumps into the water.

Pat jumps into the
water.

He jumps i--- the
water f-- the ball.

He likes it in the
w----.

The answers are on Page 48

This is fun, says Peter.

T___ is fun, he says.

We like fun.

W_ like f__ in the water.

The answers are on Page 49

Yes   No

1 Is Jane here? --.

2 Is Peter here? ---.

3 Is the dog here? --.

4 Has Peter a fish? --.

The answers are on Page 49

Yes　　No

1 Are Peter and Pat here? --.

2 Is Jane here? ---.

3 Is this a toy shop? ---.

4 Has Jane a tree? --.

Yes   No

1 Has the dog some
water? — — — .

2 Can the dog write?
— — .

3 Can toys jump? — — .

4 Have Peter and Jane
some fish? — — — .

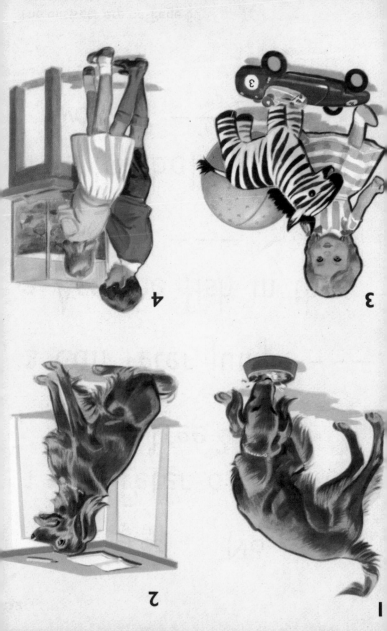

Yes   No

1 Are Peter and Jane in the tree? -- .

2 Can Peter jump? --- .

3 Are the fish in the water? --- .

4 Is the ball in the water? -- .

The answers are on Page 50

3

4

1

2

Finish the sentences with the
help of the pictures.

1 The dog wants --- ----.

2 Jane looks for --- ----.

3 Peter is in --- ----.

4 Peter and Jane look
in --- ---- .

| the fish | the ball |
| the tree | the shop |

The answers are on Page 50

1

2

3

4

Finish the sentences with the
help of the pictures.

1 Peter and Jane
like ———— .

2 Here are some ———— .

3 Peter writes to ———— .

4 Jane likes ——— ——— .

sweets	toys
Jane	the dog

The answers are on Page 50

1

2

3

Dear Jane,

4

Here are Peter and
Jane.

They want to go home.

You and I want to go
h--- , says Peter.

Yes, we want to go
h--- , says Jane.

Pat, the dog, w----
to go home.

The answers are on Page 51

Write out correctly—

1 Peter I Look, can says, jump.

2 water Jane some wants.

3 some They sweets have.

4 home Peter Jane and are.

The answers are on Page 51

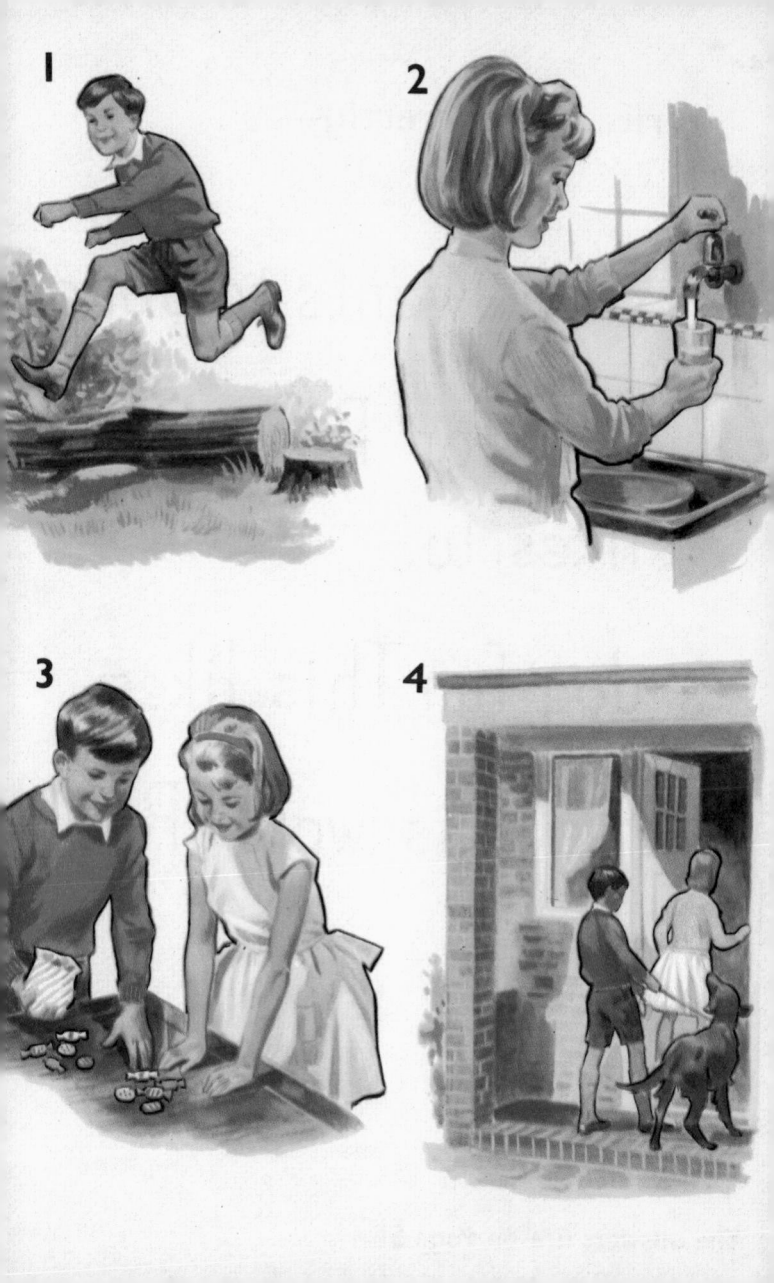

Write out correctly—

1 write wants to Jane.

2 fish for Peter look likes to.

3 dog fun This likes.

4 the in is water Pat.

The answers are on Page 51

Pages 46 to 51 give answers to the written exercises in this book. They can also be used for revision and testing, before proceeding to Book 3a.

Page 4

Peter can write.

Jane can write.

I can write.

Page 6

They can write.

They like to write.

They write for fun.

Page 8

Peter writes for fun.

Jane writes for fun.

I like to write for fun.

Page 10

Peter says, Here you are, Jane.

Jane says, Here you are, Peter.

Here you are, they say.

Page 12

Peter, have a sweet.

Have some sweets.

Have some sweets, Peter.

Page 14

I want to fish.

I want to go to the water.

I want to go to the water, Jane.

Page 16

Here comes Pat.

Here comes Pat, the dog.

Pat comes to Peter and Jane.

Page 18

Here they come.
Here comes Peter.
Here comes Jane.
Here comes Pat.

Page 20

Look here, Peter says.
Look here, he says.
The fish can jump.
Look, the fish can jump.

Page 22

The ball is in the water.
Go for it, says Peter to Pat.
Go for it, he says.
Pat jumps into the water.

Page 24

Pat jumps into the water.
He jumps into the water for the ball.
He likes it in the water.

Page 26

This is fun, says Peter.
This is fun, he says.
We like fun.
We like fun in the water.

Page 28

1 Is Jane here? No.
2 Is Peter here? Yes.
3 Is the dog here? No.
4 Has Peter a fish? No.

Page 30

1 Are Peter and Pat here? No.
2 Is Jane here? Yes.
3 Is this a toy shop? Yes.
4 Has Jane a tree? No.

Page 32

1 Has the dog some water? Yes.
2 Can the dog write? No.
3 Can toys jump? No.
4 Have Peter and Jane some
   fish? Yes.

Page 34

1   Are Peter and Jane in the tree?   No.

2   Can Peter jump?   Yes.

3   Are the fish in the water? Yes.

4   Is the ball in the water?   No.

Page 36

1   The dog wants the fish.

2   Jane looks for the ball.

3   Peter is in the tree.

4   Peter and Jane look in the shop.

Page 38

1   Peter and Jane like sweets.

2   Here are some toys.

3   Peter writes to Jane.

4   Jane likes the dog.

Page 40

Here are Peter and Jane.

They want to go home.

You and I want to go home, says Peter.

Yes, we want to go home, says Jane.

Pat, the dog, wants to go home.

Page 42

1 Peter says, Look, I can jump.

2 Jane wants some water.

3 They have some sweets.

4 Peter and Jane are home.

Page 44

1 Jane wants to write.

2 Peter likes to look for fish.

3 This dog likes fun.

4 Pat is in the water.

New words used in this book

Total number of new words 24

Pages 46, 47, 48, 49, 50 and 51 contain answers, and can be used for revision and as test pages.